FOOTBALL RECORDS SMASHED!

by Bruce Berglund

CAPSTONE PRESS
a capstone imprint

Published by Capstone Press, an imprint of Capstone
1710 Roe Crest Drive, North Mankato, Minnesota 56003
capstonepub.com

Library of Congress Cataloging-in-Publication Data
Names: Berglund, Bruce R. author.
Title: Football records smashed! / by Bruce Berglund.
Description: North Mankato, Minnesota : Capstone Press, [2024] | Series: Sports
illustrated kids. Record smashers | Includes bibliographical references and index.
| Audience: Ages 9–11 | Audience: Grades 4–6 | Summary: "In football, players
pull off some fantastic feats to clinch a win, set a record—or both. In 2021, Justin
Tucker kicked a 66-yard field goal to break the record and win the game for the
Baltimore Ravens. And no one can top the Miami Dolphins' perfect season in
1972. In this Sports Illustrated Kids book, young readers can experience these
exciting moments and other record-setting plays in football. Fast-paced and
fact-filled, this collection of record smashers will delight sports fans with
thrilling achievements in football history"—Provided by publisher.
Identifiers: LCCN 2023000032 (print) | LCCN 2023000033 (ebook) | ISBN
9781669050056 (hardcover) | ISBN 9781669050018 (pdf) | ISBN 9781669050032
(kindle edition) | ISBN 9781669050049 (epub)
Subjects: LCSH: Football—Records—United States—Juvenile literature. |
Football—United States—History—Juvenile literature.
Classification: LCC GV955 .B47 2024 (print) | LCC GV955 (ebook) | DDC
796.332/64—dc23/eng/20230112
LC record available at https://lccn.loc.gov/2023000032
LC ebook record available at https://lccn.loc.gov/2023000033

Editorial Credits
Editor: Ericka Smith; Designer: Terri Poburka; Media Researcher: Svetlana
Zhurkin; Production Specialist: Katy LaVigne

Image Credits
Associated Press: Doug Pizac, 19, File/Gregory Payan, 26, Greg Trott, 24, Mark
Zaleski, cover (front); Getty Images: David Banks, 11, David Madison, 20,
Diamond Images/Kidwiler Collection, 14, Icon Sportswire/Fred Kfoury III, 27,
Icon Sportswire/Stephen Lew, 12, Joe Robbins, 25, Los Angeles Times/Al Seib,
23, Mike Ehrmann, 28, 29, Nate Fine, 16, Nic Antaya, 9, NurPhoto/Jorge Lemus,
8, Silas Walker, 5, Sports Illustrated/Heinz Kluetmeier, 15; Newscom: Icon
Sportswire/John McCreary, 13, Icon Sportswire/Scott W. Grau, 7; Shutterstock:
EFKS, cover (back), krissikunterbunt (fireworks), cover and throughout, pixssa
(cracked background), 1 and throughout

TABLE OF CONTENTS

Words in **bold** are in the glossary.

AMERICA'S BIGGEST SPORT

Football is the most popular sport in the United States. Fans pack stadiums to watch the National Football League (NFL) teams play. NFL players break records every year. Here are some of football's greatest record smashers.

FACT

Some NFL records have lasted a long time. In 1929, the Chicago Cardinals' Ernie Nevers scored six touchdowns and kicked four extra points in one game. He scored 40 points—a record that still stands today.

THE LONGEST KICK

It's exciting when a player breaks a record. It's even better when they do it to win a game.

On September 26, 2021, the Baltimore Ravens played the Detroit Lions. With seconds left, the Ravens were behind by one point. Kicker Justin Tucker lined up for a field goal. The ball was 66 yards from the goalposts.

Tucker preparing to kick a field goal

Tucker kicked the ball. It hit the **crossbar**. It bounced straight up. Then it fell past the crossbar. It was good!

The NFL record for longest field goal had been 64 yards. Matt Prater set that record in 2013. Tucker smashed Prater's record. And he won the game for the Ravens!

GO-TO RECEIVER

On passing plays, receivers run downfield. The quarterback checks to see who is open. Most quarterbacks have a player they throw to often. That's their "go-to receiver."

In 2019, Michael Thomas was the go-to receiver for the New Orleans Saints. And he usually caught the ball.

Thomas making a catch

During a game against the Tennessee Titans, Thomas caught his 144th pass. He smashed Marvin Harrison's record for most catches in a season! He finished the season with 149 **receptions**.

The NFL named Thomas the 2019 Offensive Player of the Year after his record-setting season.

A PERFECT SEASON

The NFL has had many great teams. The 1972 Miami Dolphins stand above them all. They are the only NFL team to have a perfect season.

The Dolphins won all 14 games of their regular season. Then they won two games in the playoffs.

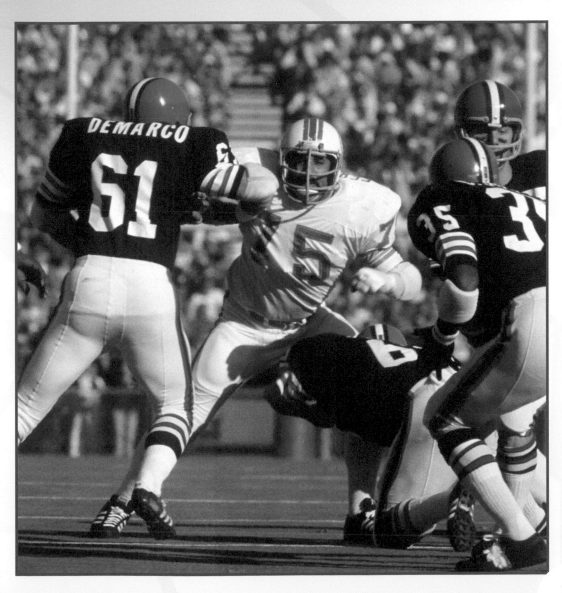

The Dolphins made it to the Super Bowl. They won that game too. The Dolphins finished the season with 17 wins and no losses—a perfect season.

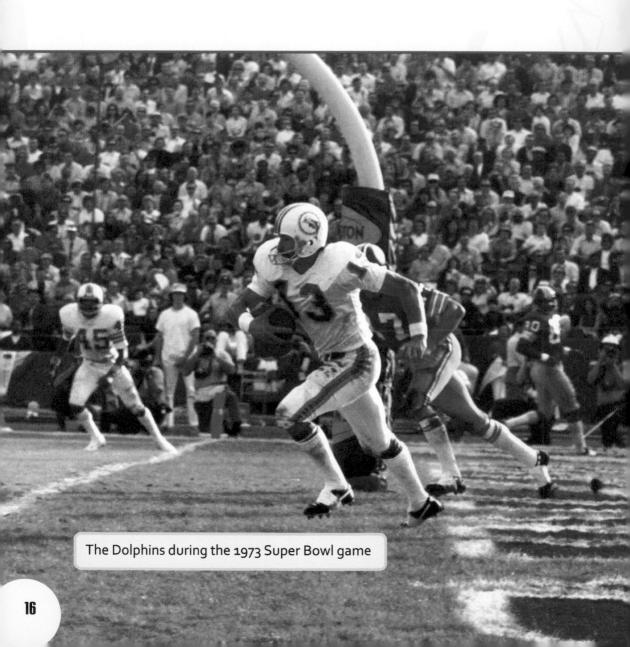

The Dolphins during the 1973 Super Bowl game

One-Loss Seasons

Since the start of the Super Bowl, five teams have finished the year with just one loss.

Team	Season	Regular-Season Record	Super Bowl	Final Record
Raiders	1976	13–1	Won SB XI	16–1
Commanders	1982	8–1	Won SB XVII	12–1
49ers	1984	15–1	Won SB XIX	18–1
Bears	1985	15–1	Won SB XX	18–1
Patriots	2007	16–0	Lost SB XLII	18–1

RUNNING FOR THE RECORD

The best running backs rush for more than 1,000 yards in a season. A few have run for more than 2,000 yards.

In 1984, the Rams' Eric Dickerson became the second player ever to rush for 2,000 yards. The record had been 2,003 yards. It had lasted for 11 years. But Dickerson smashed it in the Rams' second-to-last game of the year.

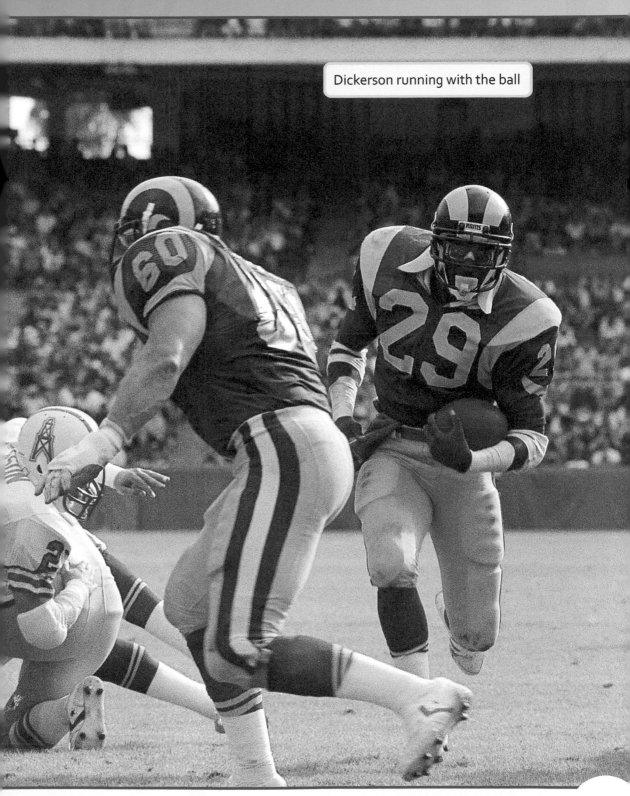

Dickerson running with the ball

After the Rams' last game, Dickerson had run for 2,105 yards. Now, more running backs have rushed for over 2,000 yards. But no one has topped Dickerson.

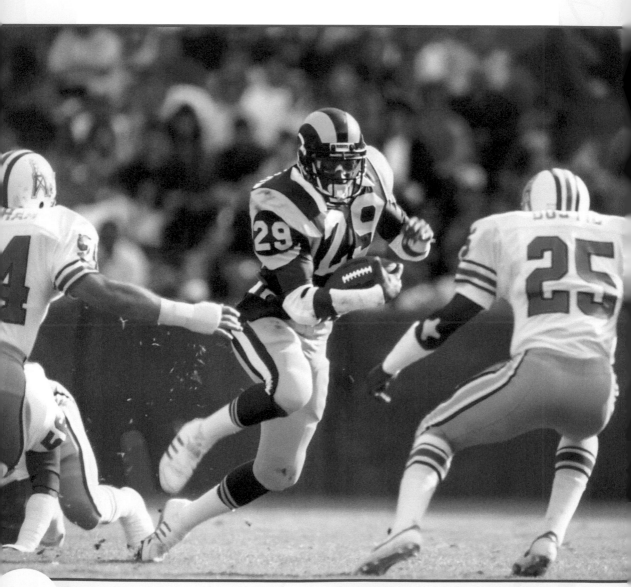

Chasing Dickerson

Six running backs have run for more than 2,000 yards since Dickerson smashed the record.

Season	Player	Team	Rushing Yards
1997	Barry Sanders	Lions	2,053
1998	Terrell Davis	Broncos	2,008
2003	Jamal Lewis	Ravens	2,066
2009	Chris Johnson	Titans	2,006
2012	Adrian Peterson	Vikings	2,097
2020	Derrick Henry	Titans	2,027

RECORD-SETTING ROOKIE

Many **rookies** have a hard time their first year in the NFL. This is especially true for quarterbacks. They must get used to faster players and trickier defenses.

In 2020, rookie Justin Herbert started as the **backup** quarterback for the Los Angeles Chargers. But the starting quarterback got hurt. Herbert started the second game. He ran for a touchdown and threw a touchdown pass.

Justin Herbert

Herbert started the rest of the season.

He had no problem adjusting.

Herbert celebrating a touchdown pass

Before Herbert, Baker Mayfield held the record for most touchdown passes by a rookie quarterback. During the 2018 season, he made 27 touchdown passes for the Cleveland Browns. Herbert finished the 2020 season with 31 touchdowns. He shattered Mayfield's record.

Mayfield throwing a touchdown pass

SUPER CHAMPION

When an NFL team wins the Super Bowl, all the players get a ring. It shows they were on a championship team.

A Super Bowl ring

When Tom Brady won Super Bowl LIII in 2019 with the New England Patriots, it was his sixth win. He smashed the old record of five Super Bowl rings. Charles Haley, who played in the 1980s and 1990s, had set that record.

A poster showing Brady with six Super Bowl rings

In 2021, Brady made it back to the Super Bowl with the Tampa Bay Buccaneers. They crushed the Kansas City Chiefs 31–9. And Brady earned his seventh Super Bowl ring. His string of wins will be hard to beat!

Brady celebrating his Super Bowl win in 2021

Brady with the Super Bowl trophy in 2021

GLOSSARY

backup (BAK-uhp)—in sports, the player who comes into a game if a starting player gets hurt or tired

crossbar (KRAWS-bahr)—in football, the metal bar between the two goalposts; the crossbar is 10 feet above the ground

reception (ri-SEP-shuhn)—in football, when a player on offense catches a pass

rookie (RUK-ee)—a player who is playing their first year on a team

READ MORE

Berglund, Bruce. *Football GOATs: The Greatest Athletes of All Time.* North Mankato, MN: Capstone, 2022.

Flynn, Brendan. *Basketball Records Smashed!* North Mankato, MN: Capstone, 2024.

Zweig, Eric. *It's a Numbers Game! Football.* Washington, DC: National Geographic Partners LLC, 2022.

INTERNET SITES

Pro Football Hall of Fame: Football History
profootballhof.com/football-history/football-history

Pro Football Reference: NFL Leaders, Football Records, NFL Leaderboards
pro-football-reference.com/leaders

Sports Illustrated Kids: NFL Zone
sikids.com/nfl-zone

INDEX

ABOUT THE AUTHOR

Bruce Berglund played baseball, hockey, and football as a kid. When he got older, he was a coach and referee. Bruce taught college history for many years. He wrote a history book for adults on world hockey. He is now writing a book about the history of referees and umpires.